ABRIDGED
CLASSICS

ABRIDGED CLASSICS

BRIEF SUMMARIES OF BOOKS YOU WERE SUPPOSED TO READ BUT PROBABLY DIDN'T

JOHN ATKINSON, creator of *Wrong Hands*

HARPER
DESIGN
An Imprint of HarperCollinsPublishers

To Dylan, Jacob, and Madz

Published in 2018 by
Harper Design
An Imprint of HarperCollins*Publishers*
195 Broadway
New York, NY 10007
Tel: (212) 207-7000
Fax: (855) 746-6023
harperdesign@harpercollins.com
www.hc.com

Distributed throughout the world by
HarperCollins *Publishers*
195 Broadway
New York, NY 10007

ISBN 978-0-06-274785-3

Library of Congress Control Number: 2017945063

Printed in China

First Printing, 2018

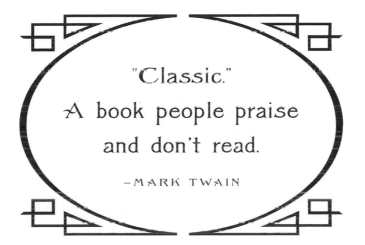

"Classic."

A book people praise
and don't read.

—MARK TWAIN

ULYSSES

James Joyce

Dublin, something, something, something, run-on sentence.

MOBY DICK

Herman Melville

Man vs. whale.

Whale wins.

BEOWULF

Unknown

Hero kills monster.
Blah, blah, blah.
Dragon kills hero.

Wait, yes he does.

WALDEN

Henry David Thoreau

Man sits outside for two years.

Nothing happens.

MACBETH

William Shakespeare

Old ladies convince a guy
to ruin Scotland.

BRAVE NEW WORLD

Aldous Huxley

Everyone is high.
Nothing gets done.

IN SEARCH OF LOST TIME

Marcel Proust

Smell of cake reminds
a guy of stuff.

Four thousand pages of stuff.

THE SUN ALSO RISES

Ernest Hemingway

Lost generation gets drunk.

They're still lost.

NAKED LUNCH

William S. Burroughs

Heroin can really mess you up.
Anyway, here's an orgy.

THE PICTURE OF DORIAN GRAY

Oscar Wilde

*If looks could kill,
they probably will.*

THE BROTHERS KARAMAZOV

Fyodor Dostoyevsky

Brothers are very contentious,
like their father.

Also Russia.

TO KILL A MOCKINGBIRD

Harper Lee

Kids don't understand racism.

Adults don't either.

THE CATCHER IN THE RYE

J. D. Salinger

Moody teen complains a lot.
He has a red hat.

THE FAERIE QUEEN

Edmund Spenser

"How Not to Be a Jerk"
for knights.

Then four legs bad.

PRIDE AND PREJUDICE

Jane Austen

Girl hates wealthy aristocrat.

Wait, no she doesn't.

THE ODYSSEY

Homer

War veteran takes forever to get home, then kills everyone.

THE ILIAD

Homer

Not the Odyssey.

DON QUIXOTE

Miguel de Cervantes

Guy attacks windmills.

Also, he's mad.

CRIME AND PUNISHMENT

Fyodor Dostoyevsky

*Murderer feels bad.
Confesses. Goes to jail.*

Feels better.

CATCH-22

Joseph Heller

War is crazy, unless you are.
Orr maybe not.

HEART OF DARKNESS

Joseph Conrad

Colonialism ruins everything.
Also jungle metaphors.

THE REPUBLIC

Plato

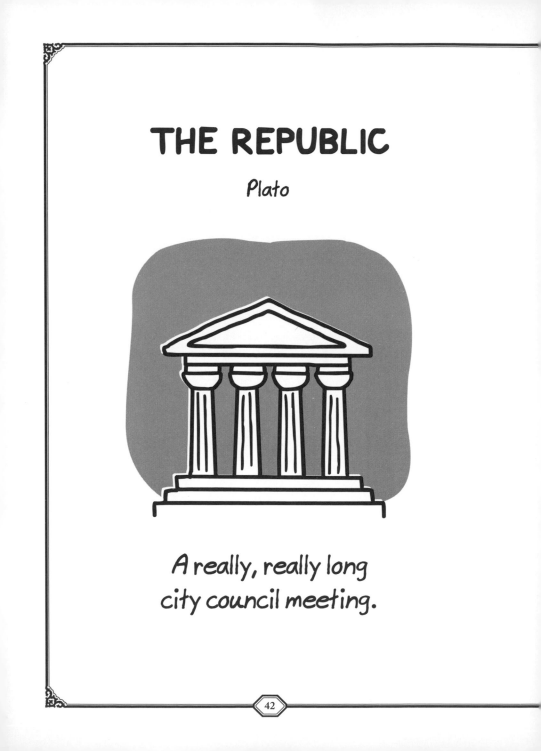

A really, really long
city council meeting.

Socrates is there.

WUTHERING HEIGHTS

Emily Brontë

A sort-of brother and
sister fall in love.

It's foggy.

ROBINSON CRUSOE

Daniel Defoe

Old-timey Gilligan's Island.

THE PEARL

John Steinbeck

Owning stuff is problematic.

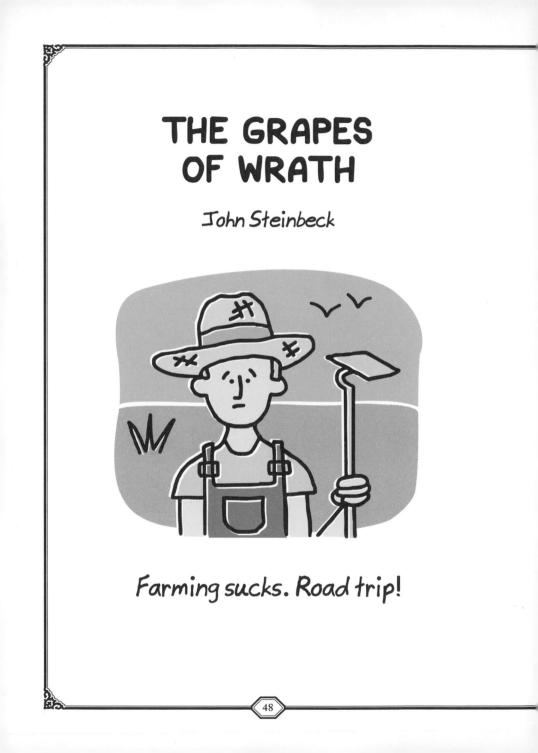

Road trip sucks.

A FAREWELL TO ARMS

Ernest Hemingway

There are no winners in war.

And very few adjectives.

THE RIME OF THE ANCIENT MARINER

Samuel Taylor Coleridge

Old sailor kills a bird,
then interrupts a wedding.

OTHELLO

William Shakespeare

A lost hankie ruins
everyone's relationship.

ON THE ROAD

Jack Kerouac

Post-war America is
complicated and depressing.

Booze helps.

THE CANTERBURY TALES

Geoffrey Chaucer

Medieval version of
"99 Bottles of Beer."

With sex and poop jokes.

THE DIVINE COMEDY: INFERNO

Dante Alighieri

All hell breaks loose.

PETER PAN

J. M. Barrie

Some kids and a crocodile
pester an amputee.

TREASURE ISLAND

Robert Louis Stevenson

Booty hunt goes awry.

Then it doesn't.
Then it does. Then it doesn't.

FRANKENSTEIN

Mary Shelley

Monsters are people too.

Pieces of people.

GULLIVER'S TRAVELS

Jonathan Swift

Hapless sailor is stranded on
different lands inhabited
by sociopolitical metaphors.

1984

George Orwell

Vision of a dystopian future (now called Tuesday).

GREAT EXPECTATIONS

Charles Dickens

Poor boy's benefactor is a crook.

Old lady is no help at all.

THE ADVENTURES OF HUCKLEBERRY FINN

Mark Twain

Kid takes a trip on a raft.
Hijinks ensue.

Also slavery.

THE AENEID

Virgil

Angry gods make guy's trip
to Italy an epic ordeal.

THE RETURN OF THE NATIVE

Thomas Hardy

*Local man comes home
and ruins everything.*

SENSE AND SENSIBILITY

Jane Austen

Two sisters catch husbands.

And one catches a cold.

THE TRIAL

Franz Kafka

Guy is prosecuted.
No one knows why.

We don't know why either.

EMMA

Jane Austen

Busybody badgers everyone
to get married.

THE LORD OF THE RINGS TRILOGY

J. R. R. Tolkien

THE FELLOWSHIP OF THE RING

THE TWO TOWERS

THE RETURN OF THE KING

Middle-earth's epic
jewelry return policy.

THE GREAT GATSBY

F. Scott Fitzgerald

Rich, selfish people hang out.

Something about
the American dream.

KING LEAR

William Shakespeare

Old king goes mad.

Everyone dies.

IVANOV

Anton Chekhov

Guy hates everything.
Gets married. Kills himself.

THE CRUCIBLE

Arthur Miller

Hunt for witches turns
into a witch hunt.

ETHAN FROME

Edith Wharton

Farmer's life can't
possibly get any worse.

Hey, a sled!

ANNA KARENINA

Leo Tolstoy

Woman has an affair.
Then it ends.

Then a train.

JANE EYRE

Charlotte Brontë

Workplace romance gets fiery.

TWELFTH NIGHT

William Shakespeare

Identity theft and cross-dressing causes confusion and marriage.

THE DA VINCI CODE

Dan Brown

Things are hidden in art.

WEDDING
RING?

Jesus things.

ROMEO AND JULIET

William Shakespeare

Teen lovers commit suicide.
Wait, no they don't.

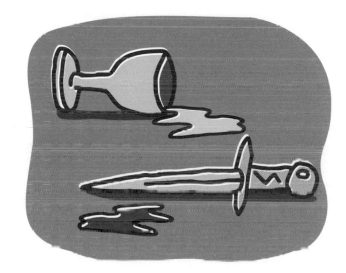

Okay, now they do.

THE MYSTERIES OF UDOLPHO

Ann Radcliffe

Gothic *Scooby-Doo*.
With lots of secret passages,
fainting, and punctuation.

THE SCARLET LETTER

Nathaniel Hawthorne

Puritan tale of adultery,
mockery, and embroidery.

LITTLE WOMEN

Louisa May Alcott

Four sisters get married.

Except Beth.

THE PILGRIM'S PROGRESS

John Bunyan

A guy named Christian walks to Heaven.

You get the idea.

MADAME BOVARY

Gustave Flaubert

Bored woman misbehaves,
then kills herself.

THE STRANGER

Albert Camus

Mother dies. Stranger dies.
Existentialism lives.

TO THE LIGHTHOUSE

Virginia Woolf

Boy wants to visit a lighthouse.

Ten years later he does.

THE METAMORPHOSIS

Franz Kafka

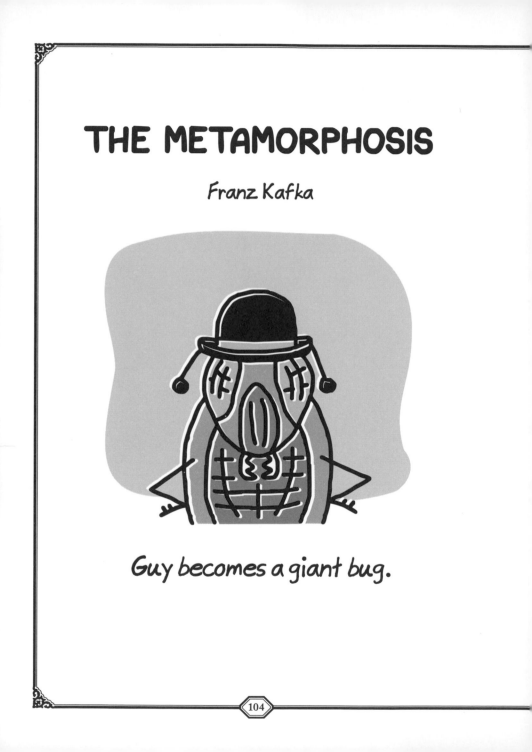

Guy becomes a giant bug.

And a metaphor for something.

WAITING FOR GODOT

Samuel Beckett

Still waiting.

HAMLET

William Shakespeare

Guy with daddy issues mopes
and whines about who to kill.

OF MICE AND MEN

John Steinbeck

Two drifters.
Dumb one kills soft things.

Smart one kills dumb things.

LOLITA

Vladimir Nabokov

Boy meets girl.

Except boy is 37 and girl is 12.

THE FOUNTAINHEAD

Ayn Rand

Architect-creep does whatever he
wants and won't shut up about it.

OEDIPUS REX

Sophocles

Patricide, incest, and
self-mutilation: the play.

THE HANDMAID'S TALE

Margaret Atwood

An oppressive patriarchy
controls women's bodies.

This book is also about that.

A PORTRAIT OF THE ARTIST AS A YOUNG MAN

James Joyce

Irish lad is torn between
the church and sex.

So he becomes a writer.

THE WONDERFUL WIZARD OF OZ

L. Frank Baum

Young girl's fanciful
ordeal over footwear.

RICHARD III

William Shakespeare

Jerk kills everyone until he's king (see also Macbeth).

PARADISE LOST

John Milton

God allows free will.

Until you mess up.
Then he banishes you.

THE LION, THE WITCH AND THE WARDROBE

C. S. Lewis

A lion eats a witch in a closet.
Some kids watch.

The lion is Jesus.

THE HUNCHBACK OF NOTRE DAME

Victor Hugo

Deformed bell-ringer
in a deformed society.

THE COUNT OF MONTE CRISTO

Alexandre Dumas

Guy escapes from jail and
kills everyone who put him there.

THE WASTE LAND

T. S. Elliot

*A modernist's plea
for a smarter society.*

In a poem that makes
everyone feel stupid.

THE RED BADGE OF COURAGE

Stephen Crane

Young soldier is a hero.
Except he's not.

Then he is.

TARZAN OF THE APES

Edgar Rice Burroughs

Ape? Man?
Ape-man!

THE BELL JAR

Sylvia Plath

Young girl tries to fit in.
She doesn't.

MOLL FLANDERS

Daniel Defoe

Thief cons everyone.
Repents. Ends up rich.

Yay?

THE THREE MUSKETEERS

Alexandre Dumas

Three guys in big feathery
hats have sword fights.

Another guy shows up.

CHARLOTTE'S WEB

E. B. White

Clever web designer saves a pig.

JULIUS CAESAR

William Shakespeare

Story of political backstabbing.
With actual stabbing.

CANDIDE

Voltaire

Life is horrible.

But gardening is fun!

THE PRINCE

Niccolò Machiavelli

How to win friends
and influence people.

Except with no friends
and killing people.

THE JUNGLE BOOK

Rudyard Kipling

Feral boy messes about in the
woods then goes home.

THE RAVEN

Edgar Allen Poe

A bird flies into some guy's house and annoys him.

LORD OF THE FLIES

William Golding

Marooned boys are bad at everything.

Except killing each other.

ANNE OF
GREEN GABLES

Lucy Maud Montgomery

Redheaded orphan's
antics bother everyone.

Then they don't.

THE OLD MAN AND THE SEA

Ernest Hemingway

Senior's dinner is
eaten by sharks.

TOM JONES

Henry Fielding

Cheeky orphan comes of age.
With silliness and naughty bits.

MRS. DALLOWAY

Virginia Woolf

Party planner's day ends
with, well, a party.

Also a suicide.

FAHRENHEIT 451

Ray Bradbury

Fireman memorizes books.
People cause problems.

The world blows up.

TROPIC OF CANCER

Henry Miller

A jerk visits Paris in the 1930s.

LIFE OF PI

Yann Martel

Boy is adrift with a tiger.
Or people. Or no one. Or God.

THE BIBLE

Unknown

Be good or else.

Acknowledgments

To the dictionary for providing the words and to all of the authors who were able to put them in an interesting order.

Index by Book

Index by Author

About the Author

John Atkinson lives in Ottawa, Canada. He is a voracious reader of cereal boxes, microwave instructions, and subtext. John is plagued by a recurring dream where he misses the Renaissance because of car trouble. He also claims to have coined the phrase, "I had a banana on the train," which everyone tells him isn't really an expression.

John's cartoon *Wrong Hands* has been featured in numerous online and print publications worldwide and can be seen regularly in *Time* magazine. www.wronghands1.com